Columbus

Admiral of the Ocean Sea

Edited by:
Beverley Birch

Production by:
John Morton

Teacher panel:
Susan Bibbings
Peter Gale
Dave Winter

Cover design:
Laurence Bradbury

Picture research:
Jenny Golden

Photograph acknowledgements:
Photo Oronoz, Madrid/Museo del Prado, 10;
Scala/Biblioteca Nazionale, Florence 8, 9.

First published 1979
Macdonald Educational Ltd
Holywell House
Worship Street
London EC2

ISBN 0 356 05915 4

Printed and bound by
Waterlow (Dunstable) Ltd.

Contents

Columbus

Admiral of the Ocean Sea

by Ronald Latham

illustrated by Chris Molan

Macdonald Educational

A boy in Genoa

In the Italian sea-port of Genoa there lived a weaver named Domenico Colombo, who had three sons and one daughter. The eldest son, Christoforo, who was born in 1451, has become world-famous as Christopher Columbus, the 'discoverer of America'.

Columbus was not, of course, the first man to visit America. In the year 1000 a Norse seaman, Leif Erikson, had sighted land south of Greenland. It must have been somewhere either in Canada or in the United States. But the Norsemen were prevented from settling in 'Vinland', as they called it, by the Red Indians, who had reached there first, thousands of years before. After that, Vinland was almost forgotten. It was from Christopher's voyage into the unknown that Europeans first learnt of the vast 'New World' across the Atlantic.

The Genoese were proud of their free city, with its splendid mansions and churches. But on land they were squeezed into a narrow strip between the mountains and the sea. Only within the circle of the city walls, guarded by strong forts, could they feel safe from their envious neighbours. It was as seamen and traders that they had grown rich and famous. So in Genoa all eyes were turned towards the sea, even those of the weaver's son, Christopher, as he worked at his father's loom.

He was always slipping out of the weaving room and down to the harbour, sometimes even out to sea in a fishing boat. Domenico soon saw that his son would never become a good weaver. So he gave him the chance of becoming a good sailor. It was a hard life, but it might cure the lad of day-dreaming.

But Christopher went on dreaming. Even in church, when he heard the priest say how Christians believed it was a noble task to teach Jesus Christ's message of peace and goodwill to those who had never heard it, he remembered that his own name, Christopher, meant 'Christ-bearer'. So he pictured himself carrying the message to strange people in far-away lands full of fabulous treasures. All his life long he never lost this dream. And sometimes he managed to persuade himself, and even other people, that it might come true. But the reality turned out to be stranger than the dream.

A shipwrecked sailor in Lisbon

By the year 1476 when Christopher was 25, he was an experienced seaman, but only along the well-charted shores of the Mediterranean Sea. That year he signed on for a voyage in a ship from Flanders (now known as Belgium). This ship was returning home by way of Portugal and England. It sailed in convoy with other ships because Flanders was at war with France. Off the Portuguese coast the convoy was attacked by a French fleet. Christopher's ship was sunk, and he escaped only by clinging to an oar and swimming to land. He made his way to the Portuguese capital, Lisbon.

For a would-be explorer, Lisbon was the most exciting city in the world. Portuguese sailors had discovered islands previously quite unknown – the Cape Verdes and the Azores far out in the Atlantic. They were venturing ever further south down the African coast, bringing back rich cargoes of gold and negro slaves. They were also developing the art of navigation, by which a man could hope to discover his position in mid-ocean by observing the sun and stars. And they were making better maps than any made before.

Christopher drank in this new knowledge. He became fluent in Portuguese, learned to speak some Spanish and to read Latin, the language in which all scientific books were written. Along with his younger brother, Bartholomew, who also loved the sea but in a less adventurous way, he started a business in Lisbon as a map-maker and book-seller. But he still made sea voyages and got to know the winds and currents of the Atlantic from Madeira northward to Iceland. In 1479 he had the good fortune to marry Felipa Perestrello, who was not a wealthy heiress but a lady of noble family. In Portugal unless you were a member of a noble family you were unimportant. People who would turn a deaf ear to the son of an Italian weaver, however much he knew about geography and navigation, might be willing to listen to Felipa's husband. For by now, Christopher's dreams were beginning to take a definite shape. He was quite sure that he could turn them into reality, if only someone of importance could be persuaded to listen to him. He had a tempting prize to offer.

Christopher and his younger brother, Bartholomew, in their map-making shop in Lisbon. Christopher's wife, Felipa, is in the background.

A short-cut to the Indies

As a weaver, Christopher knew well that the finest cloths in the world were the delicate silks and rich brocades that came from the Far East, together with spices, gems and other costly luxuries. Two centuries earlier, no one in Europe had known where these treasures came from. Then a merchant from Venice – Genoa's main rival among the trading cities of the Mediterranean – had written a book in which he described the magnificent empire of Kubilai Khan, Lord of Cathay (China), the gold-roofed palaces of Japan and the spices and perfumes of the Indies. This book, *The Travels of Marco Polo*, became Christopher's favourite.

But the overland routes by which Marco had travelled to these far-off countries were now barred to Christians by the Muslims – the followers of the prophet Mohammed. They wanted to keep these routes for their own use. The European nation that could avoid those routes by finding a direct sea route to the Far East could make itself very rich. The Portuguese had been trying to find such a sea route. In their voyages down the west coast of Africa, they were hoping to reach the southern tip of Africa, from where they could perhaps turn east and sail straight for the Indies.

But Christopher had a better idea. Why not, instead of travelling east, go the other way and sail due west from Europe across the Atlantic?

After many efforts to get an audience with King John II of Portugal, he was finally granted one in 1484. The king was impressed with Christopher's plan. But his advisers warned him against it. They believed, quite rightly, that the earth was much bigger than Columbus thought. If there was nothing but open sea between Europe and Asia, how could any ship carry provisions enough for the outward voyage, let alone for the return.

Christopher was in fact quite wrong in his calculations. His firm belief that he was right helped to convince some of his listeners, while others resented it. But he had good reason to trust in his own seamanship. He was willing to risk his life and eager to prove the truth of his theory that you could reach India by sailing west across the Atlantic.

Right: how one man imagined the world looked, based on Marco Polo's book. This map was drawn in about 1457 by Toscanelli, a mathematician and astronomer from Florence.

Columbus found support for his own plan in Toscanelli's ideas about the size of the earth.

Christopher's audience with King John II of Portugal. He explains his plans and tries to get the King's support.

Right: the real map of the world: the arrows show the different directions for reaching the Far East.

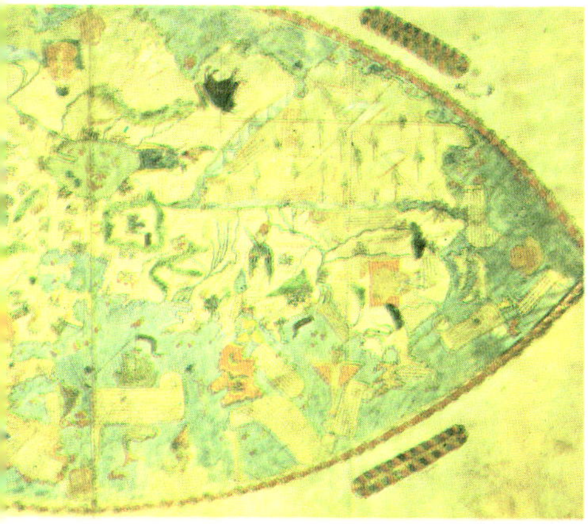

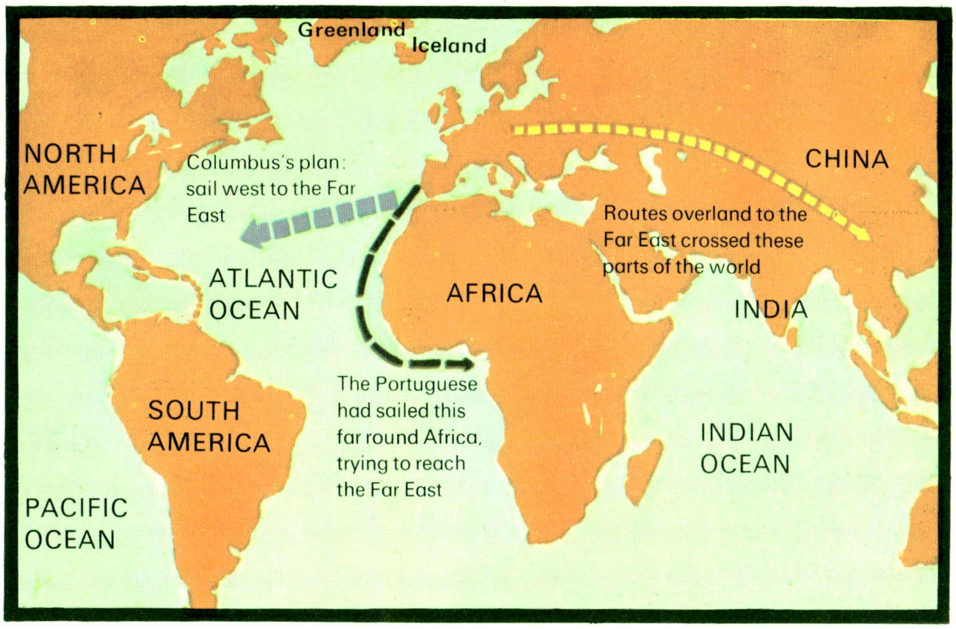

Looking for a sponsor

Above: this picture of King Ferdinand V of Aragon and Queen Isabella of Castile was painted nearly 490 years ago, while they were alive. We do not know who the artist was.

It shows them kneeling in worship of the infant Jesus Christ and his mother. Ferdinand is kneeling on the left, dressed in red robes, and Isabella is kneeling on the right in brown robes.

The 'Commissions' investigating Christopher's plans.

The first time we know for certain that Christopher met Ferdinand and Isabella was in the spring of 1486. They asked their advisers to investigate Christopher's theories and report back to them. This was called a 'Commission'.

The King and Queen's advisers said the world was much larger than Christopher believed and that no caravel or fleet could stay at sea long enough to reach the Indies by the direct route across the Atlantic. They were right, and in fact, if there had been no continent of America in the way, it is possible that Columbus would have vanished into the ocean, never to be heard of again!

For the next eight years Christopher exhausted his strength and his money in the search for someone to support his plan – a 'sponsor'. He wanted someone who would not only provide ships and crews for an expedition but who also had the authority to promise the huge reward which Columbus demanded. He wanted to be made 'Admiral of the Ocean Sea' and governor of all the islands he might discover, and be given one tenth of the money gained from them.

He sent his brother Bartholomew, without success, to put the scheme before King Charles VIII of France and King Henry VII of England. But he pinned his faith mainly on Ferdinand, King of Aragon, and Isabella, Queen of Castile. By their marriage they had united the whole of what we now call Spain except for Granada in the south. This was ruled by Muslims. It was the King and Queen's great ambition to conquer Granada. On 2 January 1492 they succeeded.

By this time Christopher, after long years spent pestering them with his demands, had given up in despair. He had tried another appeal to King John of Portugal. But John had just learned that his admiral, Bartholomew Diaz, had finally reached the southern tip of Africa – the Stormy Cape, he called it. King John, full of hope that this would open a way to the Indies, renamed it 'Cape of Good Hope'. But to Christopher it meant only disappointment, for King John was not interested in him or his plan.

He decided to leave Spain for good. With no clear idea of where he would go next, he rode his donkey slowly towards the city of Cordova. Suddenly he was overtaken by a galloping horseman. The rider carried a royal letter telling him to return urgently to the Spanish court. One of the few people who believed in Columbus's plan was the King's Keeper of the Privy Purse, Luis de Santangel. Luis thought that, after the thrill of conquering Granada, the King and Queen might be in a mood to risk this new venture. Isabella had always been fond of Columbus, the handsome foreigner with the magnificent dreams. She decided to give him his chance. King Ferdinand, with much less enthusiasm, agreed.

A messenger spurs after Columbus with a message to return to the King and Queen at Court.

Preparing for sea

On 12 May 1492 Christopher arrived at the little port of Palos. He had papers signed by the King and Queen authorising him to sail in their service to 'certain parts of the Ocean Sea'. The papers also ordered the townsfolk to provide two of the small ships called 'caravels' and equip them for the voyage. A third ship was to be hired by Christopher, who was given the authority to recruit seamen for this tiny fleet.

All this was supposed to be done in ten days. In fact it took three months of hard work. Almost everyone in town was opposed to the scheme. Luckily for Christopher, he won the support of an important family of ship-owners – the three brothers Pinzon. They volunteered to accompany him on the expedition as officers. With their help he was able to tempt 90 seamen to venture their lives on what seemed to most people to be the dream of a madman.

The three vessels of Christopher's expedition were solidly built three-masted sailing ships. Two were 'caravels' and were called the Niña and Pinta. They were probably about 20 metres long and very broad in the beam, perhaps about six metres. Christopher's flag-ship, the Santa Maria, was not much bigger. They were not very comfortable ships, even for the officers. But no one expected comfort at sea. It would be nothing new to the sailors to spend their nights on deck, wherever they could find a bit of level space. Nor would it be a new experience to live on hard-tack biscuit, salt meat or fish – fresh fish when they could catch it – and probably, since they were Spaniards, olive oil and garlic.

At the port of Palos de la Frontera, Christopher and his crews get their ships and supplies ready for their voyage into the unknown.

They were also used to running risks. But this voyage was not like any other. The Commander, Christopher, was gambling on a guess with which few people agreed. No one could foresee what dangers lay ahead. Even if we ignore the imaginary sea-monsters and other horrors which quite sensible people believed might be lurking in these untravelled waters, the sailors had good reason to wonder if they would ever see their homes again.

Into the unknown

On 3 August 1492 the three ships set sail from Palos. They were built for running before the wind; to beat up against it by tacking (that is, zig-zagging) was, at the best of times, slow and laborious and sometimes impossible. So Christopher planned to sail first to the Canary Islands, where he knew he could count on a steady east wind (the 'trade wind') to blow them on their way. In the Islands they made some necessary repairs and took on fresh water and provisions. On 6 September they were at sea again. Steering due west, they were now sailing straight out into the unknown.

By measuring the height of the sun or a star they could make a rough estimate of their distance north or south of the equator (that is, their 'latitude'). But for finding how far west from Europe they had come they could count only on 'dead reckoning' – that is, estimating how fast they had been travelling, for how long, and in what direction. This was little better than guess-work.

After two weeks sailing, the Commander let it be known that, according to his official log book, they had travelled about 400 leagues west of the Canary Islands (about 2,400 kilometres). The captains of the other two ships thought the distance was more, and by his own reckoning Christopher secretly believed that it was much more. But to the men even 400 leagues was terrifyingly far. If the east wind persisted, how would they ever get back?

And now the wind died down. They found themselves becalmed in the Sargasso Sea, where sea-weed grew so thick in the water that they were afraid they might stick in it. Christopher told them, quite mistakenly, that it must have been uprooted from shallow coastal water; so it was a sign that land was near. So were the petrels and bosun-birds that flew around them, and even, as he thought, the whales.

On 25 September, with a freshening breeze behind them, their hopes seemed confirmed. Surely that was a solid mountain rising out of the sea, black against the sunset! Could it be Antillia, the Island of Seven Cities, of which strange stories were told?

Or was it one of the magic islands that the Irish monk, St Brendan, was supposed to have visited? But alas! as they drew near, the mountain turned out to be only a cloud.

Land Ho!

After this disappointment the men grumbled more than ever. Some were openly mutinous. If their crazy commander could not be persuaded to turn back, he must be forced to – or else thrown overboard! At an angry meeting on board the Santa Maria, the loyal Pinzon brothers urged the Commander to crush the mutiny by hanging the ring-leaders. But Christopher did not need to use such violent measures. He was quite sure he knew where he was and where he was going. No one else was sure of anything. So the seamen grumbled, but obeyed the order to sail on.

On 7 October a second mountain was sighted – but again it turned out to be a cloud! But soon there were encouraging signs of land. Sticks and wisps of grass drifted by, and flights of birds passed overhead, heading southwest. The Commander agreed to alter course a little and follow them – surely the birds must know which way the land lay!

By the evening of 11 October Christopher felt in his bones that there was land to westward, and not far away.

Mutiny brews among the sailors.

Suddenly he had a clear vision of a light ahead, rising and falling, though not everyone could see it. A few hours later a signal was fired from the leading ship, the Pinta. A sailor called Rodrigo de Triana, peering through the misty moonlight, believed he had spied a white cliff. The Commander ordered the fleet to heave to and wait for daylight.

Third time lucky! The dawn brought a clear view of waves breaking on a rocky shore with wooded hills beyond. It was Christopher's big day, the fulfilment of his dream, and he wanted it to be all his own. It was rather unfair to poor Rodrigo, that, because Christopher had seen the mysterious light, he claimed for himself the reward promised by the King of Spain for the first man to sight land beyond the ocean.

In honour of Christ, the 'Holy Saviour', Christopher christened the island San Salvador. He had no doubt that it was one of the Indies – the islands visited by Marco Polo on his voyage from China to India. In a few more days, he thought, the fabulous treasures of the East would be theirs for the taking!

'Land in sight.' For nights the sailors strained their eyes through the darkness for a glimpse of land. Aboard the Pinta, the sailor Rodrigo de Triana suddenly sights what looks like a white cliff. The first land they had seen for 33 days, since they had set sail from the Canary Islands.

An island paradise

As the three ships found a safe anchorage off the shores of this beautiful and fertile island and the captains were rowed ashore in the ships' boats, the grumblers were silenced. This was a day of rejoicing. In a solemn ceremony of prayer and dedication, with the royal banner of Castile fluttering proudly in the breeze, the Commander took possession of the island in the name of 'their most Catholic Majesties, King Ferdinand and Queen Isabella, and of their divine overlord, Jesus Christ'. It was the first of many such performances by European captains in many parts of the world.

This ceremony was watched by a crowd of fascinated and bewildered natives. They were quite unable to imagine what it was all about. These pale-skinned beings, in towering canoes wafted over the water by huge wings, must surely be gods who had come down from heaven! The natives themselves, as we now know, were the descendants of immigrants from South America. They belonged to a group of tribes known as the Arawaks, who had made their way northwards from island to island in swift and sea-worthy canoes. They were gentle, good-natured people. In that climate clothes were unnecessary, so they usually went naked. Land and sea supplied all their simple wants with very little labour from them.

To Christopher, of course, they were 'Indians', and the name 'Indian' has been used ever since by Europeans to describe the many native tribes of this new-found continent. But, if these were the Indies, where were the treasures of the East? The Indians willingly gave presents, ranging from balls of cotton thread to gaily-coloured parrots, or traded them for glass beads and other novelties. But the only things that really interested the Spanish visitors were the gold rings that some men and women wore in their noses.

The Indians made signs that the gold came from the south, and they seemed to be saying 'Cubanacan', probably meaning the island of Cuba. But the sound reminded Christopher of Marco Polo's Kubilai Khan, the mighty Emperor of China. Were they getting near the source of the gold?

A strange world

So the little fleet set sail once more in search of new islands to claim for Spain and Christianity. But above all they were in search of gold. To aid the search they took some natives of the island on board. They were rather unwilling passengers. They soon picked up a little Spanish and acted as guides and interpreters.

The fleet reached the north coast of Cuba and sailed along it towards the west, far enough to make Christopher feel sure that it must be the mainland of China. When he heard of a great ruler living somewhere inland, he sent a party to call upon him, bearing a letter from King Ferdinand and Queen Isabella addressed to the Chinese Emperor. But the great ruler was just a poor Indian chief, living in a village of huts.

The Spaniards did not find what they expected. But the things they did find were remarkable enough. The only domestic animals seemed to be dogs which never barked. They were used for food. The wild animals were even stranger. A fearsome, dragon-like monster, which Christopher killed, was called an 'iguana' by the natives.

The sailors even saw mermaids – disappointingly ugly ones – rising out of the sea. We call them manatees. The plants that provided the natives with food were just as strange to the Spaniards: yams and sweet potatoes and cassava roots – bitter and poisonous till the juice was squeezed out and they were made into the starchy stuff we know as tapioca.

And what queer customs the natives had! They did not even sleep on beds, but in big nets slung from the roof. They called them *hamacas*. Sometimes they would stuff powdered leaves into little tubes or pipes (called *tobacos*), which they thrust into their noses. Then they would set light to the leaves and breathe in the smoke.

The Spaniards thought that the Indians would make good servants. But it was not worth trading with them as they had nothing of any value to sell. The islands seemed like jewels – emeralds set in a sea of sapphire. But they were not the sort of jewels that could be used to pay the cost of an expensive expedition. Even if they had reached the mainland of China, they still had to find the gold which they had promised to bring back.

Onward through the islands

One day they heard of a place to the east where gold could be picked up on the beach. So they headed back east. To Martin Alonso Pinzon, Captain of the Pinta, who had spent his whole fortune on the expedition, this was welcome news. As the Pinta was the fastest ship, he soon went ahead and lost sight of the others. It was a foolish act in these unknown waters, and Christopher was very angry. A long-lasting quarrel began between Christopher and the Pinzon family.

Christopher's fleet, now reduced to two ships, reached the island of Haiti, which he christened Hispaniola (Little Spain). Here he made friends with a helpful chief of the Taino tribe, named Guacanagarí, who gave him a cloth adorned with the face of a god made of real gold. The gold came from a rich mine in a place called Cibao. Cibao! Surely this was Cipangu, Marco Polo's name for Japan! With high hopes they set sail on Christmas Eve to skirt the towering cliffs of Cape Haitien, tacking slowly eastwards against the trade wind. It was a calm night. Thankfully, Christopher snatched the first sleep he had had for 48 hours.

Sailing in dangerous waters. The quarrel between Christopher and the Pinzon family was a sign that all was not going well. Christopher still insisted that they had reached the Indies. But he had no definite proof to offer his royal sponsors, and no way of satisfying the men who had risked everything for the sake of the glittering prizes he had promised them. Even his most loyal supporters were beginning to suspect they had been led on a fool's errand.

So far they had been very lucky. The seas surrounding these islands are full of dangers, even today, when every rock has been carefully charted. For a stranger with no maps to guide him, no knowledge of local weather conditions, no clue to where he was going or even where he was, they were bristling with death-traps. Even with Christopher's natural gift of seamanship, his experience and skill as a pilot, it is amazing they had travelled so far without serious mishap.

Below: the map of Christopher's first voyage. The white line shows the route of his ships.

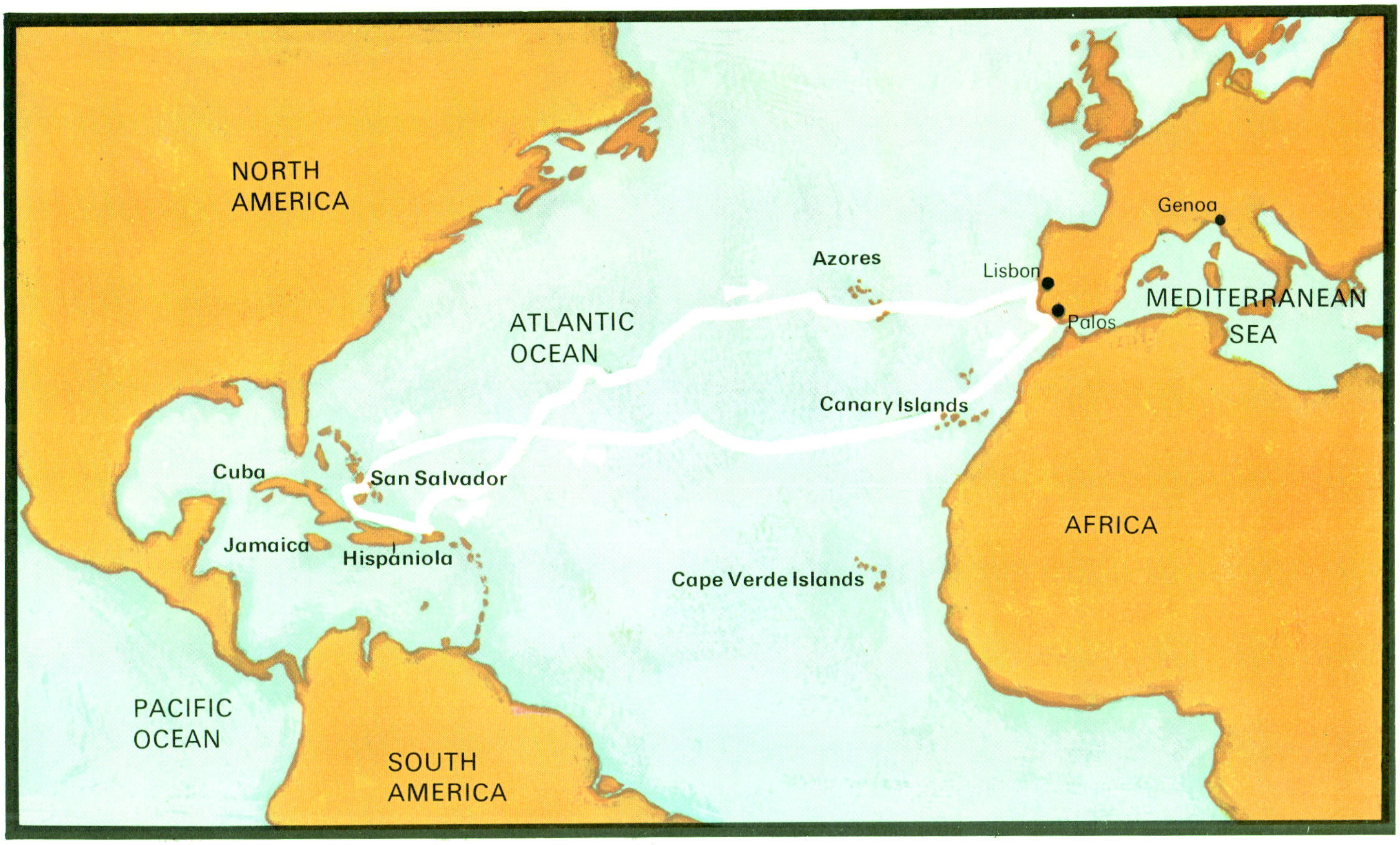

Welcomed by the Tainos in Hispaniola.

The first colony

In the early hours of Christmas morning, 1492, the Commander's well-earned sleep was rudely interrupted. The Santa Maria had grounded on a coral reef! All attempts to float her off were in vain. There was nothing for it but to abandon ship. Thanks to the willing help of Guacanagarí and his men, her precious load of stores was got ashore speedily and without loss.

But what next? It was out of the question for the whole company with the necessary provisions to be transported across the Atlantic in the little caravel Niña. Christopher quickly made up his mind that the wreck was a sign that God wanted him to establish a Christian colony in these islands, and had actually chosen the site for it. So, on the very spot where they had been driven ashore, they built a village of huts. They protected it with a stout stockade. It was to be called Villa de la Navidad (Christmas Town).

Here Christopher planned to leave a garrison of 40 men under the command of a personal friend, Diego de Harana. They had provisions for a year or more, and would await his return. Now that he had earned his title of Admiral of the Ocean Sea, he was confident that within a few months he would be sent out in command of a much larger force, to explore and govern Spain's new empire and turn its peace-loving inhabitants into good Christians.

Meanwhile, what had happened to the Pinta? There was a rumour that she had anchored in a river further to the east, and Christopher tried to send a message there. But it was not till 6 June, when the Niña had already set sail, that Martin Alonso Pinzon reappeared, full of excuses. The Commander made a show of forgiving him, but the quarrel remained unhealed.

Before the two caravels left Hispaniola, they had one final adventure. When a landing party went ashore at Samana Bay, they were greeted with a shower of arrows. The natives did not put up much of a fight. But it was a warning that there were other islanders besides the easy-going Arawaks and Tainos and they might not all be willing to submit to new masters without a struggle to defend themselves.

Homeward bound

The return voyage began well. The Commander set his course north of the direct route so that the ships were soon clear of the easterly trade winds into the North Atlantic, where they were helped by the prevailing west wind. But soon it rose to a gale of terrifying violence. The two caravels, each struggling desperately to keep afloat, were forced to part company. Christopher wrote a brief account of his voyage, which he stowed in a watertight barrel and threw into the sea. If they were all drowned, he thought, this might be the only survivor!

To the seamen on the Niña it seemed that only a miracle could save them. They vowed that, if they came home alive, one of them would make a special pilgrimage to a church of the Virgin Mary, the mother of Christ. They drew lots by means of a marked pea to decide who would be the pilgrim. Three separate pilgrimages were promised, and twice the lot fell to Christopher. Then they promised that, if they reached shore, they would all go barefoot and wearing only their shirts to the nearest shrine of the Virgin to give thanks and ask forgiveness for their sins.

Drawing lots to find who will be the pilgrim.

On the island of Santa Maria in the Azores, the sailors are arrested as they give thanks to God for their lives and ask forgiveness for their sins.

Then, on the night of 15 February they sighted land. They had reached the Azores. These islands belonged to the Portuguese, who might well think that a Spanish ship had no business to be seeking new lands in their own private waters. The local governor was suspicious and hostile. Though he allowed fresh provisions to be sent aboard, he ordered that a party of sailors who had come ashore should be arrested. He was surprised to find them in a chapel of the Virgin, on their knees and scantily dressed. Luckily Christopher had stayed on board, so he was free to protest and bargain for his men's release. But it was nine days before they could leave the Azores.

Then the tempest struck again. After all the pounding she had taken, how much longer could the stout little caravel survive? When dawn broke she was scudding towards a rocky shore, with her sails torn to shreds. But this time Christopher knew where he was. This was Cape Cintra, and behind it lay the entrance to Lisbon. In Portugal he could expect a chilly welcome at best. But he had no choice.

Home at last

When the Niña reached the port of Lisbon, her first visitor was the master of a warship anchored nearby. It was Bartholomew Diaz, discoverer of the Cape of Good Hope. He was able to understand what Christopher's voyage had achieved, and he treated him with the respect due to Spain's Admiral of the Ocean Sea.

But King John of Portugal was not sure how to act. He believed, like everyone else, that Christopher had found a short-cut to the Indies. It would be a blow to the power and wealth of Portugal if the secret passed into the hands of her rival, Spain. And it would be dangerous to insult the Spaniards by forcibly detaining their Admiral. But, as some of his advisers pointed out it would be quite easy to have him secretly murdered.

However, news had come that the Pinta had arrived safely in the north of Spain. King John realised that if Christopher was put out of the way, his place might simply be taken by Martin Alonso Pinzon. Christopher had long feared that a rival might try to steal the honour due to him, so Pinzon's arrival in Spain was disturbing news. But it may have helped to save his life.

Columbus and his cavalcade of Indians make their way to see King John of Portugal.

Or perhaps King John was a more honourable man than his advisers. At any rate, he granted the explorer a lengthy interview; he expressed interest in the evidence Christopher had brought of his discoveries, especially the strange 'Indians' (whom he graciously presented with scarlet robes). He allowed Christopher to send a report overland to Ferdinand and Isabella in Spain. So on 13 March the Niña was able to leave Lisbon, and two days later the Admiral entered Palos in Spain to a hero's welcome.

Meanwhile Martin Alonso Pinzon, who had been hoping to speak to Ferdinand and Isabella, was coldly informed that they preferred to hear the story of the voyage from their admiral in person. So the Pinta too set sail for Palos and arrived only a few hours later than the Niña. For some this must have been a happy reunion. But to Martin Alonso, already a sick man and exhausted by the strain of his stormy voyage, it was a bitter disappointment. A few days later he died. But his family remained among the most persistent of Christopher's envious and resentful enemies.

The Admiral in all his glory

Christopher's journey across Spain was triumphal. He was welcomed by Ferdinand and Isabella in their court at Barcelona and invited to sit beside them, while the assembled nobility of Spain listened spell-bound to his words. In all his boyhood dreams he could not have imagined a grander scene.

The King and Queen confirmed his titles and official positions and granted him a coat of arms. They gave him the noble title 'Don', which was also given to his brother Bartholomew (then in France) and the youngest brother James ('Diego'), who had been invited from Genoa to share the family glory. Best of all, the King and Queen fully accepted Columbus's argument that they needed to send out a large expedition as soon as possible to explore and occupy the newly-discovered lands he had told them about.

As his wife, Felipa, was by now dead, there was nothing to keep Christopher at home. As soon as he had performed the pilgrimages he had promised on the return journey, he was eager to return to the wonderful lands of which he was now to be Governor.

In order to make other Christian states accept Spain's claim to own and rule the new territories Christopher had explored, the Pope, as head of the Christian Church, was persuaded to declare Spanish rule over all non-Christian lands west of the Azores. A year later Spain and Portugal signed a treaty dividing the unexplored world between them. This did not, however, prevent Henry VII of England from sending another Genoese seaman, John Cabot, to see what lay across the Atlantic opposite Britain. Soon the other nations of Europe joined in the race.

Meanwhile, it took many busy months at the Spanish naval base of Cadiz to assemble and equip the 17 ships assigned to the Admiral, Christopher, for his new expedition. This fleet was manned by 1200 or more men – sailors, soldiers (some with their war-horses), settlers with their live-stock, missionaries (including Christopher's brother, Diego), royal officials, and gentlemen adventurers eager to make their fortunes. On 25 September 1493, the fleet set sail.

The coat of arms which was granted to Christopher Columbus. It shows the royal arms—the castle of Castile and the lion of León—together with golden islands on a green sea and golden anchors on a blue sea.

The nations of Europe seize new empires overseas.

The Spaniards were never able to rule the whole vast continent that Christopher had discovered. But their empire included almost all of Central and South America, except Brazil, which lay far enough east to fall into the Portuguese part. The Spaniards also occupied much of North America, including California, Texas and Florida.

In their race for new empires overseas, the French settled in Canada and Louisiana, the British in Virginia and New England, the Dutch in New Amsterdam (now New York).

All these nations, and the Danes as well, seized shares in the coasts and islands of the Caribbean Sea.

The Caribs

On this second voyage, they acted on information given by their Indian guides and headed more towards the south. They first sighted land in what are now called the Leeward Islands.

Here, in the island of Guadaloupe, they came across a tribe of whom they had heard the most horrifying tales. These were the Caribs, who lived by fighting. In fact the staple food of the Caribs was the flesh of their enemies.

In this island they met no Carib warriors; the men were apparently all away raiding another island. But they were sickened by the sight of grisly human remains, besides finding captive Arawak women and children who were being fattened for the pot and were thankful to be taken on board the Spaniards' ships. The nicest things in the island were the strange fruit called ananas – we know them better as pineapples.

This experience came as a shock to those who had pictured the islanders as simple, peace-loving people. Europeans had thought it was only fairytale giants who ate human flesh.

Carib men and women defend themselves with great courage against the Spaniards, who captured one of their hollow-log canoes and its occupants.

After this, wherever they came across man-eating tribes, they called them 'Caribals' or 'cannibals'. Today the Caribs, like the other native islanders, are almost extinct. But the 'Indies' explored by Christopher, besides now being called the West Indies, are still known also as the Caribbean Islands.

Off the island of Santa Cruz, or St Croix, a party of seamen, who had landed in search of fresh water, managed to capture a canoe manned by six Caribs – four men and two women. All six defended themselves fiercely with bows and arrows, and a band of warriors in full war-paint charged out of the forest in an attempt to rescue them. This was the first real battle the Spaniards had had to fight in seizing their new empire. It taught them to respect the courage of their enemies.

The Admiral decided they must hasten on without further delay. They had to see how the comrades they had left at Navidad were faring among the friendly Indians of Hispaniola. After dark on 27 November the fleet anchored off Cape Haitien and fired a gun as a signal to the garrison of the fort. There was no reply.

A new colony

The sad truth was that the fort of Navidad had been burnt down and the garrison wiped out. They had no one but themselves to blame for it. The governor Christopher had left in charge had completely lost control. The Spaniards had split up into raiding parties. They ransacked the district seeking food, women and gold. The Indians, under a chief called Caonabó, of Carib stock, had joined together to resist their oppressors. They stormed the fort and killed the Spaniards, in spite of an attempt to save them by Christopher's friend, the chief Guacanagarí.

The Admiral, Christopher, making the best of a bad job, established a new colony on Hispaniola further east. He called it Isabella, and there the settlers planted European crops. From this basc he organised exploring parties into Cibao, which, as he had now learnt, was not Japan but a mountainous region in Hispaniola. He himself led one spectacular expedition through what he called the Pass of the Gentlemen. There was certainly gold in the streams there.

The health of the settlers was badly affected by the unfamiliar diet as well as by the climate. The Admiral had already sent part of the fleet back to Spain with an appeal for more meat, bread and wine. Now, leaving the colony at Isabella in the charge of a committee with his brother, Diego, as president, he returned thankfully to where he was most at home – the sea. In his favourite ship, the caravel Niña, and accompanied by two even smaller craft, he explored and charted the difficult south coast of Cuba. He sailed far enough west to confirm his belief that this must be the mainland of China. To settle the matter beyond doubt, he got all his men to sign a statement that they quite agreed with him! He sailed round Jamaica, which he thought the loveliest island he had seen, and returned via the south coast of Hispaniola to Isabella. Here he was confronted by a terrible mess. The new settlers at Isabella were behaving just as badly as the garrison of the first colony, Navidad, had done. The only bright spot was the unexpected arrival of his brother Bartholomew on a ship from Spain.

The dream turns to a nightmare

Slaves being loaded on to a ship for passage to Spain.

It was not in fact until after Christopher's death that the Indians found a champion—the missionary priest, Bartolomé de Las Casas, who had the courage to speak truthfully about what was happening to them. But by then it was too late. The whole island race was dying out. Las Casas thought one way to lighten the Indians' burden of labour might be to transfer it to negro slaves, who had greater powers of endurance. This merely replaced one evil by another!

Today these lovely Caribbean islands provide a home for the descendents of those African slaves.

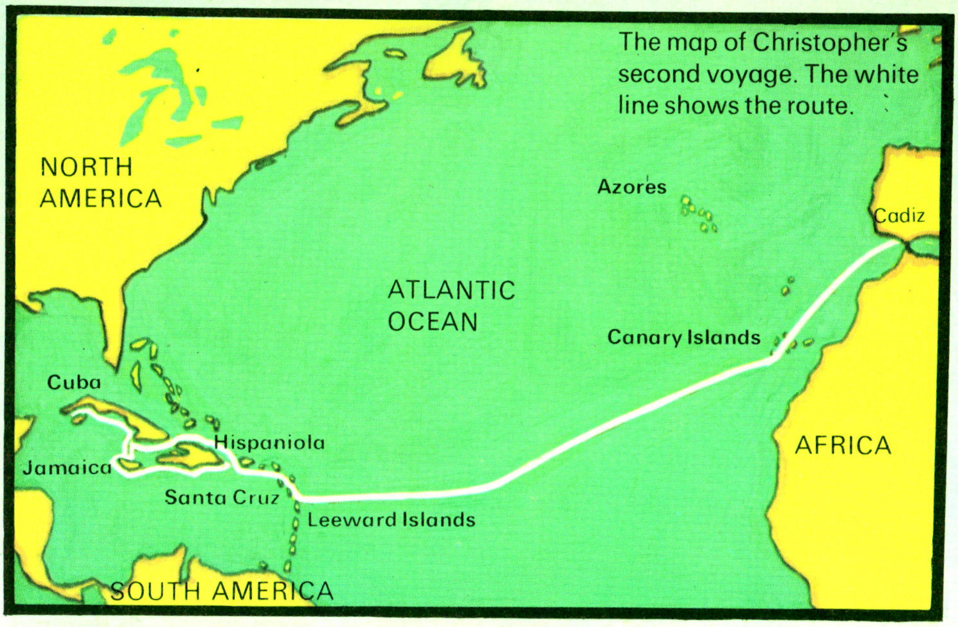

The map of Christopher's second voyage. The white line shows the route.

The Indians were helpless to resist the new settlers at Isabella. There were more of them than there had been at Navidad, and they were better armed. The most effective Indian leader, Caonabó, was captured by a simple trick: he was persuaded to put on handcuffs in the belief that they were ornaments worn by the King of Spain.

No one really wanted the settlement to succeed. The gentlemen volunteers wanted to get rich quickly and go home. Even the men who had come as settlers had no real wish to settle. Even if the Admiral wanted to stop the cruel treatment of the Indians, he was powerless to do so. Instead, he made the situation worse by imposing a tax in gold, far higher than it was possible to pay, and punishing the Indians who resisted by forced labour or even shipment to a life of slavery in Spain. This even angered the Spaniards, for they wanted profits for themselves, not for the government in Spain! Not only the fierce Caribs, but also the gentle Tainos were brutally loaded on to caravels and shipped far away from their native land. Hundreds died on the voyage.

When news of events in Hispaniola, reported mainly by Christopher's enemies, reached Ferdinand and Isabella, they sent out a Commission of Inquiry to investigate the situation. The Admiral decided to return to Spain to answer his accusers in person. He left Bartholomew behind as his deputy, with instructions to move his headquarters to a port on the south coast which he called Santo Domingo.

The homeward voyage, by a more southerly route than before, was so prolonged by head winds and calms that the crews nearly starved to death on the way.

The third voyage

Christopher appeared in the Spanish court not as an admiral but in the plain brown costume of friars and penitents. This was an acknowledgement that he was being justly punished by God for the sin of pride. But he made no excuses for his other sins. He easily disproved the accusation that he had been passing off fake gold as the real thing. And he persuaded Ferdinand and Isabella to entrust him with the command of a third expedition. This time it was much harder to attract volunteers, even though a royal pardon was offered to convicts in prison who were willing to emigrate to the 'Indies'. It was not till two years later, on 30 May 1498, that Christopher set sail. He sent five ships direct to Hispaniola, while with the three others he explored farther towards the south.

He sighted land near the southern tip of Trinidad and sailed between the island and what was in fact the mainland of South America. He had not expected to find a continent here; but he had to admit that the immense flow of fresh water from the mouth of the Orinoco River could come only from a big land mass. Further west along the coast he discovered pearl fisheries. At last a promise of real profit!

But in Hispaniola he found things no better than before. Bartholomew was faced with a rebellion – the proud Spaniards did not like taking orders from a foreigner. The brothers came to an agreement with the rebels; but after a new outbreak Christopher ordered the ringleaders to be hanged. At this moment a ship arrived from Spain. It carried Don Francisco de Bobadilla, with orders to investigate new complaints which had been made against the Columbus brothers for their high-handed behaviour.

At the sight of seven Spaniards dangling from the gallows, Bobadilla acted promptly. He ordered all three Columbus brothers to be put in chains and sent back to Spain for trial. When Christopher was brought on board, the captain wished to remove the chains. But, Christopher refused. They had been put on him in the name of his King and Queen; they must stay till the King and Queen ordered them to be taken off.

Christopher is put in chains to be sent back to Spain to stand trial.

The fourth voyage

Ferdinand and Isabella forgave Christopher for his failure to govern the unruly colony. They did not reappoint him as governor; but they yielded to his persistent appeals to be allowed one more chance to convince the doubters (including perhaps himself) that the 'New World' he had discovered was really part of the Indies.

On 3 April 1502 he set sail once more. He had four caravels, and took with him his younger son, Ferdinand, and the faithful brother, Bartholomew. At Santo Domingo the new Governor of Hispaniola, Don Nicolas de Ovando, would not let him land. He laughed aloud at Christopher's warning that the weather was unfavourable for a fleet that was just leaving for Spain. The fleet had hardly set out when it was battered to bits by a hurricane, while Christopher's caravels, berthed in a sheltered anchorage, rode out the storm.

Continuing westwards, Christopher's exploring party reached the mainland of Central America. But by the Admiral's reckoning this ought to be the Malay Peninsula to the south of China. If he followed the coast southwards he thought he would surely discover a sea-route to India. He was glad to find more signs of civilisation here than in the islands, and more gold.

On the island of Jamaica the two sinking caravels are run ashore and turned into shelters. The sailors were marooned. It was a year and five days before they could leave the island again.

But it was not a happy voyage. The weather was terrible. Many of the men were in poor health, and Christopher himself suffered from arthritis and bouts of malaria. Something seemed to be wrong with his calculations: he could not find a sea-route to India.

At Belén, not far from what is now the entrance to the Panama Canal, Christopher planned to establish the first Spanish colony on the mainland, with Bartholomew in charge. But the Indians, though willing enough to trade, had no wish to see the foreigners settling down among them. They fought back. After beating off a mass attack by Indians, in which they lost a boat-load of their men, the Spaniards made a hasty escape, leaving behind one caravel. During their long stay in tropical seas the remaining three ships had become honey-combed with holes made by boring worms. It was only just possible, by constant pumping, to keep them afloat. One ship had to be abandoned. The other two reached the north coast of Jamaica. There the crews ran them aground. They would never sail again.

Marooned

For the moment the Indians were willing to supply food in exchange for beads and other things. But this could not last. The only hope of rescue was to send a canoe party to Santo Domingo and beg aid from the unfriendly governor, Ovando. One of Christopher's trustiest officers, Diego Mendez, volunteered to make the attempt. After a harsh and difficult voyage in which some of the Indian paddlers died of thirst, he reached Hispaniola. Ovando could not openly refuse to save his fellow countrymen. But he had troubles of his own, some of them (as he believed) directly due to the arrogance of the upstart Genoese Admiral, Columbus.

Meanwhile the shipwrecked seamen on Jamaica were losing patience. Disobeying the Admiral's orders, they raided the Indian villages. One party tried to force some of the Indians to take them over to Hispaniola. But they had to give up and turn back.

The Indians stopped supplying food to men who treated them so badly. Then Christopher, who was weakened by illness and had seemed to be losing his grip, had one of his bright ideas. He called a meeting of Indian chiefs and told them that his God was angry with them. As a sign of his wrath, he would turn the colour of the moon the next night to an angry red. After that, if they refused food to the Christians a terrible punishment would fall upon them. He had noted in his almanac that on that night there would be an eclipse of the moon. The Indians were scared by this proof of the foreigner's power, and for a time the trick worked.

Four months later – a year after the landing in Jamaica – a small caravel arrived from Hispaniola. She was the only ship that Mendez, in the face of Governor Ovando's resistance, had been able to hire. But she was so rotten that she scarcely stayed afloat long enough to get the survivors back to Santo Domingo.

Even now, Christopher's troubles were not over. The hired ship in which he and his brother and son returned to Spain broke her main-mast in a storm, and the brothers had to make a substitute mast out of planks and spars. It was not until 7 November 1504 that the Admiral completed his last voyage.

This map shows the routes of Columbus's four voyages. Each voyage is shown in a different colour.

Can you match up the pictures on this map with the big pictures on the different pages in this book?

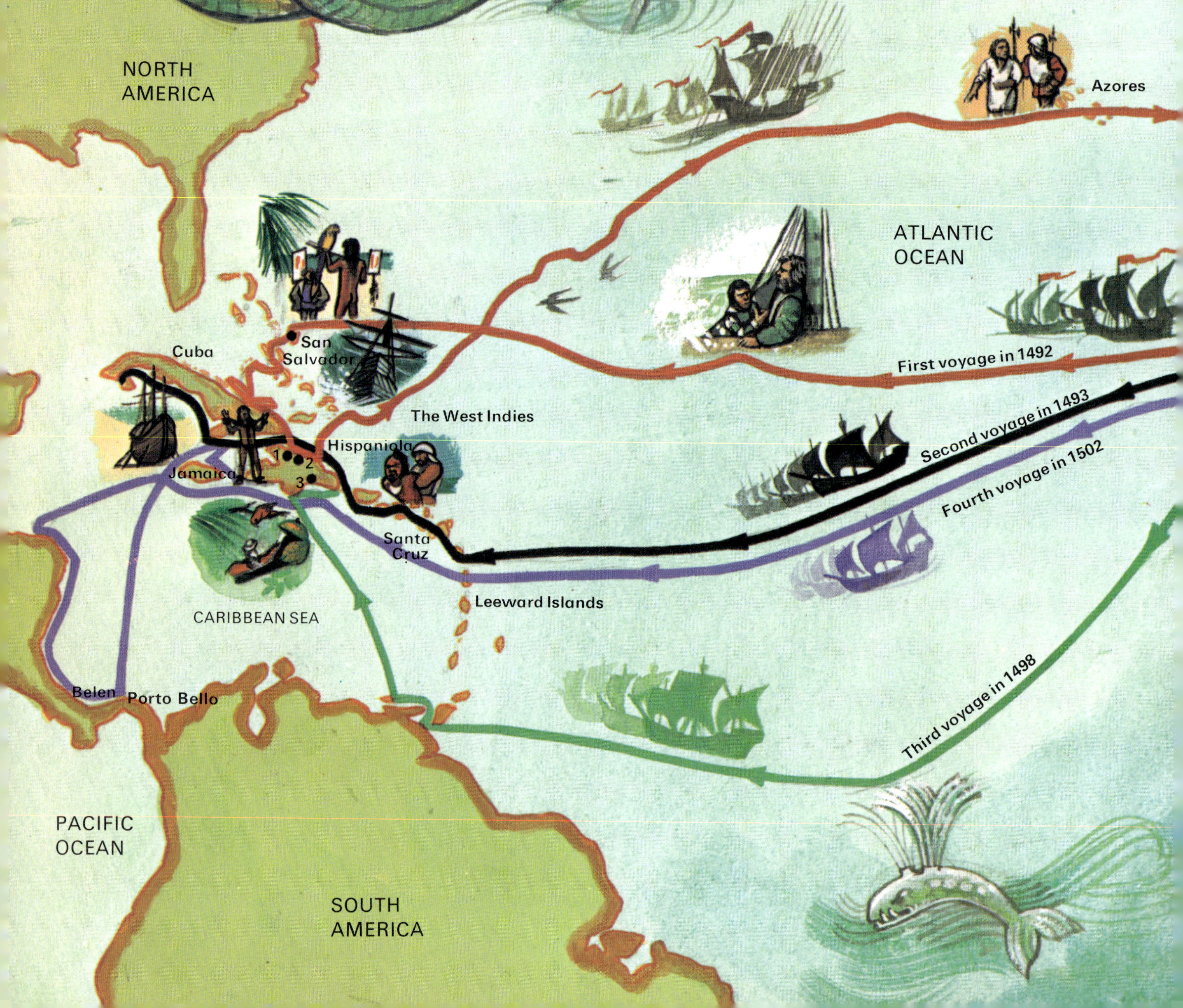

Christopher writes his will. He left most of his possessions to his elder son, Diego.

The ageing Admiral exhausted himself by continuing to claim what he believed were his rights. But by now Queen Isabella was dead and King Ferdinand had more urgent claims to deal with. When Christopher died on 20 May 1506, he felt he was a neglected man.

The new continent he had discovered was not called Columbia after him, but America after another Italian seaman, Amerigo Vespucci, who explored the coast of the southern continent further to the south. But the name Christopher Columbus is better remembered than that of any other explorer – even than Diaz and da Gama, who sailed round Africa and opened up the eastward route to the true Indies; or Magellan, who reached the Indies 14 years after Christopher's death, by finding a way round the huge land mass of America.

Christopher dreamed of glory and of gold. But even he could not have imagined the wealth that would flow into the treasury of Spain from the conquests of soldiers like Cortez and Pizarro, who seized the riches of the newly-discovered continent for Spain. He also dreamed of bringing new converts into the Christian Church. After him, others dedicated their lives to this.

But we must also remember the cruel oppression of the Indians, the destruction of their way of life and the extinction of the island tribes.

Sooner or later some sailor from Europe would have reached America. But it made a great difference to the history of the world that the journey was made at that time by a seaman in the service of Spain.

For better or for worse, Christopher Columbus transformed the map of the world.

Some important dates

1451	Birth of Christopher Columbus in Genoa.
1476	Christopher is shipwrecked off the coast of Portugal.
1476–79	Christopher lives in Lisbon, working as a map-maker with his brother Bartholomew.
1479	Christopher marries Felipa Perestrello in Lisbon.
1480–81	Christopher develops his plan to reach the Far East by sailing west from Europe.
1484	Christopher presents his plan to King John II of Portugal. It is rejected.
1484–92	Christopher's eight-year search for a sponsor for his plan.
1486	Christopher presents his plan to Ferdinand V of Aragon and Isabella of Castile, the King and Queen of Spain, for the first time.
1492	**April.** Christopher's plan is finally accepted by King Ferdinand and Queen Isabella of Spain. **August.** Christopher's first expedition sets sail from Palos de la Frontera. It consists of three ships – the Santa Maria, the Niña and the Pinta. **September.** The voyage across the unknown ocean begins. **October.** The first sight of land, at dawn. Christopher lands on San Salvador and takes possession of the island for Spain. **December.** The Santa Maria is wrecked off Cape Haitien. The fortress of La Navidad is founded.
1493	**January.** The first fighting with Indians at Samana Bay. The return voyage to Spain begins. **February.** Christopher's ship reaches the Azores. **March.** Christopher's ship reaches Lisbon, and he visits King John II of Portugal. **April and May.** Christopher is officially received by King Ferdinand and Queen Isabella in Barcelona in Spain. He is granted all his privileges and a coat of arms as reward for his discoveries. **September.** Christopher's second voyage to the West Indies begins. He sails from Cadiz with an expedition of 17 ships. **October.** The crossing of the Atlantic Ocean begins. **November.** The Spaniards fight with the Caribs at Santa Cruz. The fleet anchors off La Navidad, and they find that the garrison has been massacred.
1494	**January.** Christopher founds the second settlement, named Isabella. **March.** Christopher explores Cibao in search of gold.

1496	**March.** Christopher leaves for Spain, to answer accusations about his behaviour.
1498	**May.** Christopher's third voyage to the West Indies begins. He sets sail with six caravels.
	August. The American mainland is sighted for the first time.
1500	**August.** Bobadilla arrests the three Columbus brothers and sends them back to Spain to stand trial.
	December. The King and Queen of Spain order the release of the Columbus brothers and receive them at Court.
1502	**May.** Christopher begins his fourth voyage. He sets sail from Cadiz with four caravels.
	June. Christopher's fleet is refused permission to enter the harbour at Santo Domingo.
1503	**June.** Christopher and his crews are marooned on Jamaica.
1504	**February.** The total eclipse of the moon with which Christopher frightens the Indians.
	June. Christopher and his crews are rescued from Jamaica and return to Santo Domingo.
	September. Christopher sets sail from Santo Domingo on his final return voyage to Spain.
	November. Queen Isabella dies.
1506	**May.** Christopher dies at Valladolid in Spain.

Some important names

These are some of the most important names of places and people mentioned in this book. You can find them on the pages listed below.